New Vanguard • 104

Cromwell Cruiser Tank 1942–50

David Fletcher & Richard C Harley • Illustrated by Peter Sarson

First published in Great Britain in 2006 by Osprey Publishing,
Midland House, West Way, Botley, Oxford OX2 0PH, UK
443 Park Avenue South, New York, NY 10016, USA
E-mail: info@ospreypublishing.com

A CIP catalogue record for this book is available from the British Library

ISBN 1 84176 814 6

Page layout by Melissa Orrom Swan, Oxford, UK
Index by Alan Thatcher
Originated by The Electronic Page Company, Cwmbran, UK
Printed in China through World Print Ltd.

06 07 08 09 10   10 9 8 7 6 5 4 3 2 1

For a catalogue of all books published by Osprey Military and Aviation
please contact:

NORTH AMERICA
Osprey Direct, c/o Random House Distribution Center, 400 Hahn Road,
Westminster, MD 21157, USA
E-mail: info@ospreydirect.com

ALL OTHER REGIONS
Osprey Direct UK, P.O. Box 140 Wellingborough, Northants, NN8 2FA, UK
E-mail: info@ospreydirect.co.uk

www.ospreypublishing.com

Authors' note

The authors would like to acknowledge the help of John Church, John Wilke
Mike A. Taylor, Andrew Talbot, Timo Tuominen and Zdenek Cizinsky.
All photographs are courtesy of The Tank Museum, Bovington.

Artist's note

Readers may care to note that the original paintings from which the colour
plates in this book were prepared are available for private sale. All reproduct
copyright whatsoever is retained by the Publishers. All enquiries should be
addressed to:

Peter Sarson, 46 Robert Louis Stevenson Avenue, Westbourne, Bournemou
BH4 8EJ

The Publishers regret that they can enter into no correspondence upon this
matter.

CROMWELL CRUISER TANK 1942–50

GENESIS

Before he left France in the summer of 1940, Brigadier Vyvyan Pope sent an urgent letter to a colleague at the War Office in London. One key paragraph read, 'We must have thicker armour on our fighting tanks and every tank must carry a cannon. The 2-pdr is good enough now, but only just. We *must* mount something better and put it behind 40 to 80mm of armour.' Pope, who was Lord Gort's advisor on armoured fighting vehicles at General Headquarters of the British Expeditionary Force, had the letter delivered by hand. Things had gone so badly in France that Pope was not even certain he would get home.

If it sounded like a counsel of despair it probably was, but Pope had learned some unpleasant facts in France. Unfortunately he was too late; the next generation of cruiser tanks was already on the stocks. Granted, both the Covenanter and Crusader (see New Vanguard 14) were up-armoured as an emergency measure, but nothing could be done about the gun; not at that stage anyway. With the country stripped of tanks following events in France and under imminent threat of invasion, it made more sense to continue production of existing types than risk the inevitable delays of producing new ones. In any case, there was the demand from the Middle East to consider. It has been estimated that losses in France arrested tank development in Britain by two years, and what applied to tanks was equally true of anti-tank guns.

An improved anti-tank gun, a 57mm weapon known as the 6-pounder, was ready for production in 1939. But, again due to events in

Muffled against the cold, the crew of this early production Cavalier await the arrival of the king and queen at a site on Cannock Chase. Her Majesty will unveil the name CROMWELL, which was the original title for this tank.

France, nothing could be done until November 1941 and even then priority went to towed anti-tank guns rather than guns for tanks. And to jump ahead briefly, it is sad to record that Vyvyan Pope never lived to see the new gun in a tank. He was killed in an air crash in October 1941 and the first 6-pdr Crusaders did not reach the Middle East until the summer of 1942.

A curiosity of Pope's letter is the emphasis he appears to give to the importance of thicker armour over a better gun. Covenanter and Crusader were already in the design stage when war began and the 2-pdr was the only gun available. This is excusable. What is not is that these tanks were designed without the ability to up-gun built in. Such is typical of the lack of technical acumen and the laissez-faire attitude that infested the War Office in those early days.

Cavalier Type B tanks modified to the OP role at No 8 AFV Depot in Leicester. They are being kitted out for service with 65th (Highland) Medium Regiment, Royal Artillery.

Even so, Pope's words hit home and very soon after the fall of France in July 1940, the War Office issued basic specifications for a new cruiser tank with up to 75mm (2.95in) of frontal armour and a 1524mm (60in) diameter turret ring. No actual gun was mentioned although the 6-pdr was an obvious choice. Lurking in the wings, however, was a hideous alternative, a triple mounting comprising a 2-pdr anti-tank gun, a 3in howitzer and 7.92mm BESA machine gun – a tank gunner's and loader's nightmare. And that was not all.

Hovering in the background, like ghosts at the banquet, stood Colonel Sir Albert Stern and his Special Vehicle Development Committee, or 'The Old Gang' as they were known. These survivors of the original tank design programme of 1915, most well past retirement age, had already perpetrated two crimes against the British Army in the bulky shapes of the super-heavy breakthrough tanks TOG 1 and 2. These had failed at enormous cost, but their designers would not go away and, although it conflicted with their own ideas of future tank design, offered specifications for a cruiser tank that were forcibly promoted by Stern.

In the end common sense prevailed and the project quickly slimmed down to three contenders. These were:

Vauxhall Motors for a Cruiser Tank based on an infantry tank design they were already working on – the Churchill.

Nuffield Mechanization & Aero for what was, in effect, an improved Crusader.

Birmingham Railway Carriage & Wagon Company (BRCW) for a design like Nuffield's offering, but lighter and with their own preference of suspension and tracks.

It takes time for such designs to evolve, but even so one senses a peacetime lack of urgency in the fact that they were not considered until a Tank Board meeting on 17 January 1941. By this time the Department of Tank Design had somehow become involved with the Nuffield project and it is probably no surprise that it was their proposal, with the General Staff specification number A24, that was accepted. An initial order for six tanks was placed on 29 January and the firm was told that the new tank must be in production by the spring of 1942.

This may go a long way to explain why the Nuffield project was accepted. Despite the debacle in France the previous year, British cruiser tanks were making their presence felt in North Africa. Even as the Tank Board was meeting, cruisers of 7th Armoured Division were tearing across the trackless wastes of Cyrenaica to head off, and ultimately destroy, a huge Italian Army retreating around the coast. Inspired by both this and a new sense of urgency, the Minister of Supply and his Tank Board selected the tank that, as far as possible, was based on existing components. In their view this eliminated the need to work through the tedious and time-consuming stages of prototype testing; one simply produced a handful of pilot models in order to check details and then swung straight into production.

Geoffrey Burton, as Director of Tanks and Transport, agreed that this was a short cut, but only to disaster; he was overruled. He could have made his case a lot stronger had he realized that the Crusader itself was seriously flawed.

CAVALIER DESCRIBED

Cruiser Tank Mark VII, A24 Cromwell, as it was first known, looks at first glance like a child's sketch of a tank. A simple, rectangular hull surmounted by a boxy turret with the requisite gun sticking out the front and a series of big wheels along the side. Gone was any attempt to give the tank that sleek, racy look of Crusader. Virtually every surface was either vertical or horizontal and although it was only 152mm (6in) taller than Crusader the visual effect was of something a lot bigger. It was also longer and wider than Crusader, which was essential to accommodate the larger-diameter turret ring required to receive the bigger gun and allow for recoil. This was the big problem.

In keeping with Royal Armoured Corps doctrine, gun mountings in British tanks had free elevation. That is to say when the gun lock was released the gun pivoted on its co-axial mounting, slightly breech heavy, so that it could be moved up and down with ease by the gunner. This design was dictated by the requirement that British tanks should be able to fire on the move and it meant that the gunner, gripping the gun mounting and with his knees slightly bent, acted as a human stabilizer, balancing the gun against the movement of the tank as it raced across country. With his forehead pressed against the brow pad of the sighting telescope and one hand on the power control of the turret traverse gear, he could track his target, fire and hit it on the move. At the same time his fast-moving tank should prove a difficult target for the enemy to hit. And there is nothing wrong with that, as doctrines go, always provided that the gunner has been given sufficient time, and practice ammunition, to hone his skills, and the tank itself can be relied upon.

Since Cavalier, as it became, and Centaur and Cromwell were physically similar, this first model will be covered in detail and only the differences noted when the others are described. Much will be obvious from the illustrations, but what cannot be seen so clearly is the way the tank was divided up inside. From front to back the hull contained four unequal compartments, separated by incomplete bulkheads that acted as internal stiffeners. The front compartment was the smallest, and stepped to conform to the seated attitude of the driver on the right and hull machine gunner on the left. A short, longitudinal bulkhead divided these two. Amidships was the fighting compartment into which the turret fitted and the bulkhead behind that acted as a firewall between the crew and the engine compartment. A final bulkhead separated the engine compartment from the transmission and final drives.

Armour

British practice on armour originally favoured homogeneous plate, the type best suited to resist attack by capped armour-piercing shot as used by the Germans. The Germans preferred face-hardened plate, which was better at keeping out plain AP shot. British armour quality was not all it might have been in 1941 and plate over 35mm (1.37in) thick tended to flake from the back under impact; thus the hull front and visor plates on the new cruisers were made up from two thinner plates. The sides were also double layered, as they had been on Crusader, with the Christie suspension units sandwiched between the inner and outer plates.

Fully stowed Cavalier ARV Mark I. Ahead of it the big Caterpillar D8 tractor represents an earlier period of tank recovery. Visible stowage includes Hollebone towing bars at the rear, front jib arms to the left and the tow cable with snatch blocks.

Gun and turret

The turret was little more than a six-sided box constructed in a similar manner to the turret on Covenanter or Crusader, with an inner shell of welded plate to which was bolted an external skin of thicker armour. The Department of Tank Design was still struggling with the concept of welding armour plate and for the present favoured riveting. However, the turret was built this way to avoid the need for a frame and rivets that, if hit from outside, could fly around inside just like bullets. The bolts, by contrast, were enormous things with huge, bevelled caps that stuck out like carbuncles on the outside. The main armament was the new Ordnance QF rifled 57mm, 6-pdr Mark III, the first version designed for use in tanks. It was mounted co-axially with a 7.92mm BESA air-cooled machine gun and a sighting telescope (No 39 Mk IS) on the left. A second BESA was placed in the hull, to the left of the driver and in the roof of the turret was a breech-loading 2in bomb thrower used primarily to launch smoke rounds.

The gun mounting was unusual to the extent that it employed an internal mantlet behind a relatively large, square opening in the front of the turret. It was never popular with tank crews, who believed that the shadow created by the aperture provided the enemy with an aiming point, although this was probably a piece of tank crew mythology.

Engine, transmission and suspension

Mechanically Cavalier was identical to Crusader, although an improved version of the Nuffield Liberty (the Mark IV) engine delivered greater horsepower at higher revolutions. A multi-plate clutch carried the drive to a five-speed and reverse gearbox and then through Wilson two-speed epicyclic steering gear to the final drive reduction and finally to the drive sprockets. Gearshift and steering brake controls were pneumatically operated. Suspension was simply a stronger version of the Crusader's

Christie system that Lord Nuffield had introduced into Britain. To allow for the additional weight Nuffield's engineers reduced the length of the swing arms, which meant that Cavalier gave its crew a much bumpier ride than its predecessor. The tracks were manganese steel, dry pin skeleton type 355mm (14in) wide and 101mm (4in) pitch – 124 links per side.

CAVALIER PRODUCTION

Tank production in Britain worked on what was described as a Parentage system. The Parent was the company with overall responsibility for a particular tank. In the case of Cavalier this was Nuffield Mechanization & Aero. The Parent had two types of sub-contractor. Some provided components, and as far as Cavalier is concerned the only one worth noting was Morris Motors Ltd who provided the Liberty engines. The other firm, Ruston & Hornsby Ltd of Lincoln, manufactured complete tanks.

Production of Cavalier does not seem to have been pressed with serious effort. Indeed it was December 1941 before the prototype was ready for gunnery trials at Lulworth. Back in August it had been claimed that the Naval Land Equipment (Nellie) programme had affected Cavalier production, but the problem seems to have been the turret, which clearly was not ready until December. Within weeks, early in the New Year, it was agreed to cut production back to 500 tanks – for reasons that will become clear. In March 1942 the first pilot model was at Farnborough for trials and the Cavalier programme was now running four months late. By this time, too, the problems with Crusader were manifest, with endless complaints emanating from the Western Desert theatre. Cavalier's faults were identical: water cooling, fan drive and engine bearings. Sent back to Nuffield's for remedial work the prototype then suffered a major engine failure. Not yet satisfactory was the verdict of the Mechanization Experimental Establishment.

Cavalier's fate was sealed at a meeting of the AFV Liaison Committee on 13 February 1943. Things had moved on quite a bit by then and it was agreed that, unlike its rivals, the A24 Cruiser would not be adapted to

Winston Churchill is shown a Cromwell IV of No 2 Squadron, 2nd Welsh Guards, in March 1944. Notice how this regiment kept all markings as low down as possible, making them less eye-catching to the enemy. The aptly named *Blenheim* was the squadron commander's tank. The fitting on top of the turret is a PLM mounting, lacking its machine guns.

take the new 75mm gun nor the 95mm howitzer. Final production would be 160 tanks with 6-pdr guns and the balance of 340 to be completed as Observation Post (OP) tanks. This decision meant that the tank had been written off as a combat type but was still deemed suitable for an important auxiliary role.

Observation Post Tank

The OP Tank was a mobile signal station that operated in the front line passing information back to gun batteries in the rear. It looked like any other tank, but it was in fact a sheep in wolf's clothing. In a fast-moving battle situation it was invaluable, able to summon artillery support at a moment's notice in response to a difficult situation. It was operated by the Royal Artillery and carried a FOO, or Forward Observation Officer. The 'office' was the turret from which the 6-pdr gun was removed to make more space, although the BESA was retained and a dummy gun fitted to disguise its special role.

The turret contained two No 19 and one No 18 wireless sets with seats for the commander and operator. The front machine-gun position was removed and here was located an auxiliary charging engine, three sets of extra batteries and three cable reels. The exhaust and silencer for the charging set – either the Tiny Tim or Chore Horse model – were located on the hull roof. Brackets for the cable reels were mounted on the rear mudguards. Outwardly the only other modification was an extra aerial on the turret.

Armoured Recovery Vehicle

Following a decision by the War Office Recovery Committee that a protected towing vehicle was required to move disabled tanks from the battlefield, an Experimental Recovery Section tested a range of turretless tanks for this role. The general principle was to provide an armoured recovery vehicle for each class of tank, so a prototype Cavalier ARV duly appeared. The towing powers of these tanks were limited so a

Although the vehicle here is in fact an OP tank, this photograph provides a good view of a Cromwell Mark IV with Type F hull in post-1948 condition. Prominent on the turret is the All-Round Vision cupola, late-style vane sight and turret stowage boxes.

system of blocks and tackle was carried to enhance power. The tank also carried a portable jib and hoist to handle heavy components. In the event the Cavalier ARV was abandoned as rapidly as the tank it would have supported.

ENTER ROLLS-ROYCE

The next stage in the Cromwell saga represents the only truly inspirational moment in the wartime British tank story, and it was due to what might be called the old boys' network of the British motor industry. Henry Spurrier, third in line in the Leyland Motors dynasty, was critical of official British policy on tank design, particularly in respect of engines. Leyland Motors was already deeply involved in tank production and Spurrier related his fears to W.A. Robotham of Rolls-Royce; the result was remarkable. Robotham was head of the Rolls-Royce experimental department, which the war had effectively sidelined. Taking a fresh look at the problem Robotham and his team came to the conclusion that their magnificent aircraft engine, the V12 Merlin, could be modified to suit tanks. The result was the 600hp Rolls-Royce Meteor.

The Ministry of Supply (MOS) was so proud of this development that it published a book about it at the end of the war. A chart comparing the two engines showed that the main modifications involved removing the supercharger, changing the gear case and adding a belt drive for cooling fans and accessories. It sounds ideal, but there was a problem. Although the MOS controlled tank production, aero engine manufacturers like Rolls-Royce came under the Ministry of Aircraft Production (MAP). The Meteor shared 80 per cent of the Merlin's components and MAP's insatiable demand for Merlins meant that Meteor production continually fell behind schedule, which affected Cromwell production until an MOS manufacturer, Henry Meadows Ltd, began producing Meteors in 1944.

For trial purposes Meteor engines were installed in two Crusader tanks in May 1941. Running against the clock one tank was believed to have reached 80km/h (50mph), but it also became clear that Robotham's team

een at the Rolls-Royce Clan oundry at Belper, Derbyshire, August 1943 this is the xperimental Cromwell Pilot D, hich displays the frontal ppliqué armour, wider acks and, of course, the elded turret.

still faced a major problem. A means had to be found to ensure adequate cooling for the powerful engine. Cavalier's radiators, sandwiched between the engine and fuel tanks, would have needed 80hp (13 per cent) of the Meteor's output to cool them. Rolls-Royce developed a new layout of transverse radiators with a highly efficient fan drive that only absorbed 32hp (5 per cent) while ramming air through the engine compartment at the incredible rate of $509.7cm^3$ $(18,000ft^3)$ a minute. Added to that was the problem of transmission. The system adopted for Cavalier, derived from Crusader, was simple but wasteful of power and in any case far more sophisticated types now existed. The most promising was designed by Henry Merritt of the David Brown tractor company. It was a triple differential steering system with a five-speed and reverse gearbox that provided the tank with a range of turns depending on the gear selected, and a neutral turn (where the tank spins on its axis with one track turning in each direction) instead of the cruder skid turns.

Cruiser Mark VIII A27M Cromwell

It would have made a lot of sense to apply the new engine and transmission to Cavalier, but Lord Nuffield would not hear of it. Major alterations would have been required to the original design but this was not impossible and production could have been speeded up. Yet Lord Nuffield insisted and he was indulged. His company spent the next two years producing 500 totally useless Cavaliers.

Inevitably, however, Cromwell was almost indistinguishable from its predecessor at first glance. Built by BRCW the first example was actually running by January 1942, and following extensive trials it was declared to be 'exceptionally good' by those responsible. Not, it has to be said, that this necessarily meant very much in view of what else was available. Nevertheless, things looked so promising that by May 1942 it was agreed that production of Cromwell must be expanded and, as a result, more firms were drawn into the group.

This expansion brought with it certain problems due, according to one commentator, to 'obstinate practices'. Few are actually specified but the impression is given of firms, set like concrete into reactionary Victorian habits, that could not be persuaded to change with the times

From this elevated angle there is a good view of the Vauxhall-designed turret and the A33-style driver's hatch on one of the two single-skin welded Cromwell hulls from BRCW. The tank was photographed at Chertsey sometime in 1943.

nor, indeed, on account of the war. One example will suffice: that of a steelworks in the north-east of England producing armour panels for the front plates of Cromwell. These proved to be so poor that 100 of the new tanks were immediately fitted with the red warning triangle to inform would-be users that they were not adequately armoured.

Diversity of suppliers appears to have lain at the root of the problems. Faced with a vast increase in demand for armour plate, the relevant authority, the Iron and Steel Control, brought together an odd assortment of small producers that they referred to as The Cromwell Pool. None of these firms had the capacity to run the whole gamut of armour plate production, but they could all play a part. Thus plate from one steelworks would go to another for heat treatment, a third for rolling and so on. The initial result was a chronic muddle, compounded by desperate variations in quality, which took a long time to sort out.

Cromwell had an anticipated top speed of 64km/h (40mph) that, for a 26.5-tonne (27-ton) tank implied some serious punishment to the suspension. The designers therefore decided to double up the springs on all road-wheel stations and incorporate shock absorbers on all but the central suspension units on each side. A return to longer suspension arms compared with Cavalier meant that the Cromwell gave its crew a much more comfortable ride. As Cromwell improved and received heavier suspension, springs were strengthened and on some Marks wider 393mm (15.5in) tracks were fitted to better spread the weight.

Cruiser Mark VIII A27L Centaur

Centaur might well be described as a throwback. Having brought W.A. Robotham on board and encouraged the development of the Meteor, Henry Spurrier and Leyland Motors now expressed doubts about the possibility of providing adequate cooling for the Rolls-Royce engine. In July 1941 they abandoned the project. In the light of subsequent events this was not just a foolish decision: it was idiotic of the authorities to agree to it.

Leyland Motors was not lost to tank production; the General Staff agreed to a compromise whereby Leylands would produce a tank similar to Cromwell that took the old Nuffield Liberty engine, now in an improved model, the Mark V. A curious result of this was the requirement that

One of the participants in the Fighting Vehicle Proving Establishment Three Thousand Mile Trial. A welded Cromwell Mw, it lacks appliqué armour, hence the additional ballast to make up the weight. This view also reveals the tow hook and rear smoke emitters.

Cromwell tanks, starting with the second pilot model, should be capable of accepting the Liberty engine, as Centaur was of taking the Meteor. Thus where there was one, now there were three, all known as Cromwell at first. Ultimately they entered service as:

Cruiser Tank Mark VII A24 Cavalier (originally Cromwell I)
Cruiser Tank Mark VIII A27L Centaur (originally Cromwell II)
Cruiser Tank Mark VIII A27M Cromwell (originally Cromwell III).

L and M signify Liberty and Meteor engines respectively.

Centaur was not simply a Cromwell tank with a Liberty engine, there were numerous detail differences. For example Centaur employed the worm-operated track tensioning system adopted for Crusader and Cavalier where Cromwell used a ratchet wheel and lever. Likewise Centaur did not require the additional air intake and armoured cover on the rear deck, and since it was lighter at the rear than Cromwell it lacked the extra springs on the last two wheel stations and only had three shock absorbers on each side to Cromwell's four.

As will be seen, Centaur was never accepted as a front-line tank and even before the trials that finally condemned it an official announcement was made to the effect that the first 300 Centaurs would only ever be regarded as training tanks while the next 166 would all have to be reworked. With hindsight the entire Centaur project was a complete waste of time and material, and this at a critical period in British history.

The hybrids

Given the shared features it is tempting to imagine that converting a Centaur to a Cromwell was simply a matter of switching engines, but naturally it was not as straightforward as that. It was done, but only as a means of examining the possibilities and resulted in a few early Centaurs being fitted with Meteor engines and taking designations Cromwell Mark III or Cromwell Mark X. They were put through a series of trials in 1942.

In early 1943 English-Electric broke ranks with the Centaur Group of manufacturers and joined the Cromwell Group. They continued building tanks with Centaur hulls and suspensions, but fitted them with Meteor engines, clutches and fan drives, delivering these newly built vehicles as Cromwell Marks III or IV depending on armament. This took some of the pressure off BRCW, freeing them to continue development of Cromwell and Challenger.

THE GUNS

If the gun is what the tank is all about, then the Cromwell and its cousins were caught at an awkward stage of gunnery development. When the new tanks were being developed the cruiser was regarded as a tank fighter, but experience in the desert changed all that. Rommel's use of tanks mixed with anti-tank guns brought forth a cry for a dual-purpose weapon: one that could fire high-explosive (HE) in addition to armour-piercing (AP) shells.

The original 6-pdr for tanks, the Mark III, was a 43-calibre (length) weapon, which firing Armour Piercing Capped Ballistic Cap (APCBC) could penetrate 56mm (2.18in) of armour at a range of 1,828m (2,000yd). It was superseded, in 1943, by the longer Mark V that had a similar performance, but neither could fire an effective HE round. This problem was solved temporarily by Vickers who reamed out the 57mm gun to 75mm and chambered it to take the American ammunition used in Sherman tanks, both HE and AP. Unfortunately what was gained with HE was lost in terms of armour piercing. The best this gun could do, firing a 6.3kg (14lb) APCBC shot, was 50mm (1.97in) of armour at 1,828m (2,000yd).

CROMWELL FAMILY MAIN ARMAMENT PERFORMANCE 1941–54

Weapons	Armament for:	Ammunition	Muzzle m/sec (ft/sec)	Penetration in mm (in) at 30 degrees velocities to vertical			
				457m (500yd):	915m (1,000yd):	1371m (1,500yd):	1828m (2,000yd):
2-pdr Mks IX or X	Triple mounting with 3in howitzer and BESA M.G., proposed for A24 but not adopted	AP AP HV/T	792 (2600) 853 (2800)	58 (2.28) 64 (2.52)	52 (2.05) 57 (2.24)	46 (1.81) 51 (2.01)	40 (1.57) 45 (1.77)
6-pdr Mk V	Cavalier I, Centaur I, Cromwell I, II and III	APC APCBC APDS	862 (2830) 822 (2700) 1188 (3900)	75 (2.95) 81 (3.19) 131 (5.16)	67 (2.64) 74 (2.91) 117 (4.61)	55 (2.17) 63 (2.48) 108 (4.25)	52 (2.05) 56 (2.20) 90 (3.54)
95mm Mk I	Centaur IV, Cromwell VI and VIII	HEAT	327 (1075)	110 (4.33)	110 (4.33)	–	–
75mm Mks V or VA	Centaur III, Cromwell IV, V, Vw, VIIw, VII, A33E1 and E2	AP M72 APC M61	618 (2030) 618 (2030)	76 (2.99) 66 (2.60)	63 (2.48) 60 (2.36)	51 (2.01) 55 (2.17)	43 (1.69) 50 (1.97)
76mm M1A1	US 76mm proposed for A34, but not adopted	APC M62 APCR M93	792 (2600) 1036 (3400)	93 (3.66) 157 (6.18)	88 (3.46) 135 (5.31)	82 (3.23) 116 (4.57)	75 (2.95) 98 (3.86)
17-pdr Mks II and VII	A30 Challenger and SP2 Avenger	APCBC APDS	884 (2900) 1203 (3950)	140 (5.51) 208 (8.19)	130 (5.12) 192 (7.56)	120 (4.72) 176 (6.93)	111 (4.37) 161 (6.34)
77mm Mk I	A34 Comet	APCBC APDS	792 (2600) 1120 (3675)	110 (4.33) 178 (7.01)	105 (4.13) 150 (5.91)	91 (3.58) 131 (5.16)	89 (3.50) 122 (4.80)
20-pdr Mk 1	FV4101 Charioteer	APCBC APDS Mk 3	1019 (3346) 1430 (4692)	196 (7.72) 295 (11.61)	183 (7.20) 277 (10.91)	169 (6.65) 260 (10.24)	156 (6.14) 243 (9.57)

The free elevation arrangement already described was fine given a properly trained gunner, but it made the task of firing HE more difficult and in any case demanded a well-balanced gun. This could not be achieved with the hybrid 75mm, so a crude system of geared elevation was employed, which some believed gave the worst of both worlds. Yet this was not the gun the army wanted. In March 1942 Vickers-Armstrongs had offered a new, high-velocity 75mm gun with a 50-calibre barrel and there was a general belief that this would fit the new cruiser. It took until May 1943 to learn that it would not. Thus, with time pressing, it was the modified 6-pdr or nothing if the Cromwell was to carry a dual-purpose gun.

Meanwhile, there had been developments elsewhere. Experience in the desert showed that the old concept of close-support, with a breech-loading mortar firing only smoke rounds, was antiquated. In 1942, in keeping with the typically British skill at improvisation, a new gun was created by combining the breech of the Royal Artillery's beloved 25-pdr with the barrel liner of the 3.7in anti-aircraft gun. The result, known as the 95mm howitzer, proved to be a remarkable weapon. Firing a respectable HE shell it had a maximum range of 5,486m (6,000yd); firing High Explosive Anti-Tank (HEAT) rounds it could theoretically penetrate 110mm (4.32in) armour at any range it could reach.

Both guns had been standardized for Cromwell and Centaur by February 1943. The most interesting result of these changes was that no Centaur or Cromwell went to war mounting the 6-pdr gun. This was a pity since, with the introduction of Armour Piercing Discarding Sabot (APDS) ammunition in June 1944, the Mark V gun proved to be an excellent anti-tank weapon at close range. It could penetrate 108mm (4.24in) of armour (which even over-matched the Tiger's front plate) at 1,371m (1,500yd) and at any range up to 1,828m (2,000yd) was second only to the legendary 17-pdr.

MARKS AND TYPES

The sub-division of any given model of tank by Marks is, and has always been, common practice world wide. Each succeeding Mark normally indicates some change in gun power, armour or other physical development. In Britain, at least up to the advent of Chieftain, these Marks

CROMWELL FAMILY PRODUCTION TOTALS 1942–45

Manufacturers	Cavalier	Centaur	Cromwell (riveted)	Cromwell (welded)	Challenger	Comet	A33 'Excelsior'	Avenger	Totals
BRCW Co. Ltd			256	123	200			80	659
English-Electric		156	803	1		276	2		1238
Harland & Wolff		125							125
John Fowler & Co.		529	274			150			953
Leyland Motors		643	735			610			1988
LMS Railway Co. Ltd		45							45
Metro-Cammell			300			150			450
Morris Motors		138							138
Nuffield M&A	203	150							353
Ruston-Bucyrus		35							35
Ruston & Hornsby	300								300
Vauxhall Motors				2					2
Grand Totals	**503**	**1821**	**2368**	**126**	**200**	**1186**	**2**	**80**	**6286**

CROMWELL FAMILY MARKS AND TYPES

CAVALIERS Nuffield Mechanization & Aero, and Ruston & Hornsby

Marks	Types	Main Armament	Notes
	A, B	6-pdr Mk III or V	Riveted hull, bolted turret, 355mm (14in) tracks
I	A	6-pdr Mk III or V	Trials vehicle with 394mm (15.5in) tracks. No series production

CROMWELLS BRCW, Metropolitan-Cammell, English-Electric and Vauxhall Motors

Marks	Types	Main Armament	Notes
	A, C	6-pdr Mk III or V	Riveted hull, bolted turret, 355mm (14in) tracks
V	C	75mm Mk V	ditto
VI	C, D, E, F	95mm Mk I	ditto
'Pilot D'	similar to riveted Type A	6-pdr Mk III	Pilot welded double-skin hull, welded turret, appliqué armour, large canister springs and 394mm (15.5in) tracks
'Cromwell II'	similar to riveted Type B	6-pdr Mk III	Pilot welded single-skin hull, composite cast/welded turret, large canister springs and 394mm (15.5in) tracks
VwD	Dw	75mm Mk V	Production welded hull, bolted turret, appliqué armour, large canister springs and 355mm (14in) tracks
VwE	Ew	75mm Mk V	Similar to Cromwell VwD but low-speed final drives
VIIwE	Ew	75mm Mk V	Similar to Cromwell VwE but heavy-duty front axles and 394mm (15.5in) tracks

CENTAUR GROUP TANKS Centaurs only: Harland & Wolff, LMS, Mechanization & Aero, Morris Motors and Ruston-Bucyrus
Centaurs and Cromwells: English-Electric, Fowler and Leyland Motors

Tanks	Marks	Types	Main Armament	Notes
Centaur	I	A, B, C	6-pdr Mk III or V	Riveted hull, bolted turret and 355mm (14in) tracks
Centaur	II	not known	6-pdr Mk III or V	Designation reserved for Centaur with 394mm (15.5in) tracks No series production
Centaur	III	C, D	75mm Mk.V	Riveted hull, bolted turret and 355mm (14in) tracks
Centaur	IV	C, D	95mm Mk.I	ditto
Cromwell	X	A	6-pdr Mk III or V	Existing Centaur I converted for trials with Meteor engine
Cromwell	III	A, C	6-pdr Mk III or V	New production Centaur I built with Meteor engine
Cromwell	IV	C, D, E	75mm Mk V	New production Centaur III built with Meteor engine. Cromwell track adjuster on vehicles built to FS (Final Specification) standards
Cromwell	VI	D, E	95mm Mk I	New production Centaur IV built to FS standards with Meteor engine and Cromwell track adjuster
Cromwell	IV	F	75mm Mk V	New production Centaur III built to FS standards with Meteor engine and Cromwell suspension and track adjuster

REWORKED CROMWELLS Reworked by Royal Ordnance Factories, post-1945. (Original manufacturers BRCW, English-Electric, Fowler, Leyland and Metro-Cammell)

Marks	Hull Types	Main Armament	Reworked from:
7	C, D, E, F	75mm Mk 5	Cromwells 4, 5 and 6 No appliqué armour
7w	Dw	75mm Mk 5	Cromwell 5w Appliqué armour retained
8	D, E, F	95mm Mk 1	Cromwell 6 No appliqué armour

Riveted Cromwells Marks 4, 5, and 6 were reworked with large canister springs and 394mm (15.5in) tracks, low-ratio final drives and late-pattern trackguards. Some Type Cs were converted to Type Ds. Modified (push-out) driver's hatch fitted to all riveted Types C, D and E. Centaur track adjuster was replaced by Cromwell type.

Continued on page 16

FV4101 CHARIOTEER		Robinson & Kershaw Ltd	
Marks	**Hull Types**	**Main Armament**	**Converted from:**
6	D, E, F	20-pdr Mk 1	Cromwell 6
7	D, E, F	20-pdr Mk 1	Cromwell 7
7w	Dw, Ew	20-pdr Mk 1	Cromwell 7w
8	D, E, F	20-pdr Mk 1	Cromwell 8

Cromwell Mark 6s were reworked to Mark 8 standard during conversion. All Type Cs were converted to Type Ds. All riveted Types D and E were modified with Cromwell 7w driver's escape hatches.

usually showed up as visual differences that could be recognized by those in the know.

Cromwell, Centaur and even Cavalier to some extent were unusual in having a separate system of Types that indicated other modifications that cut across the succession of Marks and were not always instantly recognizable. Full details of all Mark and Type variations will be found in the accompanying tables, but notice that they are not random: combinations of Mark and Type relate to particular manufacturers. Variations are highlighted in captions, but three might be mentioned here as general illustrations. Type B was one result of firing trials carried out against a sample Centaur tank at Shoeburyness. These revealed a number of vulnerable points, one of which was the hatch above the front hull machine-gunner's position. It was difficult enough to open and squeeze through at the best of times, but it was also easily fouled by the turret, making it impossible to open at all, especially in an emergency. The revised design involved replacing the hatch with a door that opened sideways, moving part of the roof with it. Nobody could describe this as a vast improvement, but it worked well enough and tanks thus modified were classified as having Type B hulls. Of course, in order to clear space for the hatch to open, one external stowage locker was deleted.

Naturally the problem repeated itself on the driver's side, but it was not possible to mirror the hull gunner's hatch because certain engine controls were in the way. Once modifications had been introduced it resulted in the Type F hull, which reached the troops in the summer of

Chosen to illustrate the Great Swan, this shows a Polish Cromwell racing past a Jeep and an abandoned PaK 43, 88mm anti-tank gun. The tanks move on one route, coating one another in great clouds of dust while support vehicles use a parallel lane.

CROMWELL FAMILY WD NUMBERS and MANUFACTURERS

WD No Ranges	Tanks, Marks & Types	Manufacturers
84618–84620	Cavalier IA (pilots)	Nuffield Mechanizations & Aero
120415–120689 188657–188681	Cromwell IC, VIC, VID, VIE, VIF	Metropolitan-Cammell Carriage & Wagon Co. Ltd
121150–121406 121701–121822 121863	Cromwell IA, IC, VC. Cromwell VwD, VwE, VIIwE	Birmingham Railway Carriage & Wagon Co. Ltd (BRCW)
129620–130119	Cavalier IA, IB	Nuffield Mechanizations & Aero, and Ruston & Hornsby Ltd
130120–130164	Centaur IA	LMS Railway Co.
171762–171766	Centaur IA (pilots) Cromwell X (pilots)	Leyland Motors and English-Electric
183800–186510	Centaur IA, IB, IC Centaur IIIC, IIID Centaur IVC, IVD. Centaur III AA.I Centaur Dozer	Gun tanks by English-Electric, Fowler, Leyland, Harland & Wolff CS and AA tanks by Fowler Dozer conversions by MG Cars
187501–188082	Cromwell IVD, IVE, and VIE	Gun tanks by Leyland and Fowler CS tanks by Fowler
188151–188656 188687–188926	Cromwell IVF	English-Electric, Leyland and Fowler
189400–190064	Cromwell IIIA, IIIC, IVC, and VID	Gun tanks by English-Electric CS tanks by Fowler
217801–217880 218001–218562	Centaur IIIC Centaur III AA.I Centaur Dozer Centaur Taurus	Morris Motors, Nuffield M&A, and Ruston-Bucyrus Dozer and Taurus conversions by MG Cars
255310	Cromwell VwE	English-Electric
271901–272100	Challenger I	BRCW Co. Ltd
334901–335308 335331–336108	Comet IA, IB	Leyland, Fowler, English-Electric and Metropolitan-Cammell
348560–348639	SP, 17-pdr, Avenger	BRCW Co. Ltd

1944. Meanwhile some of the older Types were retro-fitted with a new driver's hatch with flaps split diagonally; the rear flap simply dropped into place. In an emergency the driver pushed open the front flap and knocked the rear one aside as he baled out.

Not all Type modifications were improvements. The early riveted tanks were weighted to the limit of their suspensions and the addition of new operational equipment made them overweight. The Tank Board reluctantly approved a 50 per cent reduction of engine-compartment armour to compensate and this change was introduced on hull Type C.

Welded Cromwells

The Cromwell would change in many ways, but the most significant development was welded construction, which was first considered in December 1941 – even before the riveted pilot models had been completed. Welding offered several advantages including faster production, improved protection and a watertight hull for wading. The first welded Cromwell was Pilot D built by BRCW. Its hull followed the Type A layout and it also had a welded turret, wide tracks and a new,

Open for business, a Cromwell Type E Command Tank of Headquarters 22nd Armoured Brigade, 7th Armoured Division photographed in 1945. Both turret weapons are dummies, and bent to prove it. There is a mass of intriguing detail in this picture.

large canister spring suspension permitting a weight increase to 28.4 tonnes (28 tons).

BRCW had great difficulty welding Pilot D's double, homogenous front plates, but when Machineable Quality armour became available they built two further welded hulls with thicker, single hull plates. These new hulls followed the Type B layout, but also had an improved driver's escape hatch based on the A33 Assault Tank, as well as wide tracks and large canister springs. These hulls then went to Vauxhall Motors of Luton who, in 1942, had been instructed to build Cromwells instead of Churchills. Vauxhall completed them with a new composite turret featuring cast sides and a welded roof, but the resulting Cromwell II never went into production. Churchills proved successful in Tunisia so production was to continue and Vauxhalls would build no more Cromwells.

Yet the Tank Board still required welded Cromwells and told BRCW to build as many as possible without disrupting Challenger production. This was achieved when BRCW designed adjustable hull assembly jigs that meant that both types could be built interchangeably.

Even so there was indecision about the final form of these Cromwells. In August 1943 Pilot D was fitted with appliqué armour, increasing its frontal protection to 101mm (3.97in) and setting the pattern for a Stage I design with a welded turret. A Stage II design called Commodore was also proposed with 101mm (3.97in) of single-thickness armour. Neither was built. Instead BRCW modified their Vauxhall hull with a Type D engine deck and Pilot D's appliqué armour while retaining the bolted turret and built 123 Cromwell Vw and VIIw to that design.

GOING WEST

Throughout the period when these new cruiser tanks were being developed, British tanks were coming in for a barrage of criticism. As early as July 1942, the Director, Armoured Fighting Vehicles (Major-General

Richardson AWC) was pointing out to the Tank Board the similarities between Centaur and the disgraced Crusader, and the fact that so far the Merritt-Brown transmission had been an unmitigated disaster on Churchill. He also reminded the Chief Engineer Tank Design (Robotham) 'neither the Government, War Office nor the Ministry of Supply could weather another storm such as the one we have just passed through …'

Late in February 1943, the Tank Board decided that Vickers-Armstrongs should turn their tank-building capacity over to Cromwell with the proviso that if in six months' time the tank should prove unreliable, production should be cut and America asked to supply more tanks. As late as September 1943 another senior officer wrote 'the most disturbing feature of the Cromwell tank is the fact that its inherent design will not permit the fitting of a better gun than the medium velocity 75mm'. There is no doubt that the Americans agreed. In March 1943 their General Somervell was urging Britain to stop making tanks altogether and accept American types in the interests of uniformity and reliability, although he did admit that Cromwell was better than Sherman in some respects. This request was not acceptable as far as Britain was concerned, although there was a general tendency to cut back tank production in Britain and take more from the USA as the war progressed.

As the attached tables show, many late-production Centaurs were completed as Cromwells, but none of this seems to have had any effect on Lord Nuffield. The Tank Board had compelled him to build Centaurs instead of more Cavaliers, possibly hoping for Cromwells in the long term, but he was still not reconciled with the Rolls-Royce engine. Instead he offered something called the Democrat, which sounds suspiciously like the Liberty by another name. Two were installed in Centaurs for trials early in 1944, but they showed no improvement over Meteor.

In the spring of 1943 six Centaurs and one Cromwell were shipped over to the USA. Only the Cromwell was complete, the Centaurs going without engines. This shipment was in connection with the Tank Engine Mission to the United States, headed by Sir William Rootes. Ford Motors had developed a new V-8 and were anxious to interest the British. Four of the Centaurs were to be tested with the new V-8, with two more laid aside for a proposed V12. The Americans were not impressed with the

ooking immaculate, even down a polished muzzle brake, this a Cromwell OP of 6th rmoured Division, seen outside e Battery Workshops after the ar. Notice that it retains its ormandy Cowl.

British tanks at all. The Cromwell let the side down so badly that General Richardson wrote a scathing report in which he described the British as 'the world's worst salesmen!' The Americans fitted one of the Centaurs with their latest gun stabilizer but it was not adopted, and neither was the Ford engine. Compared with the Meteor it was underpowered and in Centaur or Cromwell the Ford would not be interchangeable with the Liberty or Meteor. In spite of this, Leyland continued to argue in favour of the Ford engine until the Tank Board ruled it out in July 1943.

TRIALS AND TRIBULATIONS

The first production Centaurs and Cromwells began to replace Covenanters in 9th Armoured Division in April 1943, although some regiments had to wait until September for their first Cromwells. Both types were still under development, so the first tanks issued were built to prototype standards. Crews soon discovered that the Centaur was no more reliable than the Covenanter. Its clutch was weak and the Liberty engine sprayed oil over the radiators, causing overheating. Cromwell's Meteor was less troublesome, but both types suffered from gearbox and steering defects.

Worse still, the delivery ratio of Centaurs to Cromwells was five to one and this alarmed the divisional commander, Major-General D'Arcy. On 27 June he complained that while he understood that Centaur was only a stop-gap until sufficient Meteors were produced for the Cromwell to replace it, that policy did not appear to be accepted on the production side. He considered that Cromwell would develop into a first-class tank but that Centaur would be a second-rate one, and reported that his 129 Centaurs had received 95 defect reports, including 23 clutch failures, while only three of his 26 Cromwells had given trouble of any kind. Centaur required far more maintenance and, because it was under-powered, its Liberty engine had to work flat-out all the time. Summing up he asserted that 'any attempt to saddle the fighting troops with an indifferent fighting machine for the sake of some consideration other than military, when a first-class machine can be produced, would be criminal',

Raising the jib on a Cromwell ARV I. The tank reverses until the wire, linking track and jib, raises the latter in the correct place, when the man on top will secure the stay. A chain hoist is secured to the jib, there is a vic on the hull front and the BESA machine gun is still in place.

and he asked for the policy to be unequivocally clarified. The War Office duly obliged him with the hardest test it could devise, short of committing both tanks to battle.

Operation *Dracula*

As titles go Operation *Dracula* seems to have been calculated to invite the ribald wit. In fact it probably derived from the title of the initiating officer, Major-General Richardson, the Director, Royal Armoured Corps or DRAC (previously the DAFV). Richardson had been posted to Washington by the time *Dracula* began in August 1943, but the man who mattered was the trials officer, Major Clifford. *Dracula* involved a comparative test in the form of a 3,700km (2,300-mile) tour in which Cromwell, Centaur, Sherman III (M4A2) and Sherman V (M4A4) tanks could be tested for reliability as they roamed around the country visiting

Centaur Taurus 17-pdr Gun Tractor, one of nine converted by MG Cars of Abingdon. The full-length sand guards were designed for Cromwell, but were very rarely seen on gun tanks.

armoured formations. Thus it could also be seen as a familiarization tour for the new types while, as a by-product, it was also used to try out the effectiveness of new items of tank-crew uniform.

Operation *Dracula* could have been the kiss of death for Cromwell and Centaur. Both tanks performed badly when compared with their American counterparts, and the Centaur was so bad that Clifford announced that he would not wish to take it into combat. Cromwell showed up well for its top speed, when it was running well, but for pure reliability and staying power the M4A2 diesel Sherman took the palm.

Yet, although time was running out, both British tanks won a stay of execution while their designers strove to cure the mechanical problems. In November 1943 ten each of the latest Centaurs and Cromwells were subjected to a punishing 4,827km (3,000-mile) reliability trial in the abrasive mud of Long Valley, Aldershot. The Cromwells emerged with flying colours but the Centaurs failed again.

That was enough for the Tank Board, who declared that in the short term the battleworthy Cromwell should continue to be produced up to the limit of Meteor engine production. Centaur production would be scaled back from 2,700 to just 2,000 tanks and in May 1944 it was revealed in the press that 'Britain's latest monster tank' had been removed from the Secret List. As this was a tank that had not yet seen action, the House of Commons began to ask awkward questions, not just about Centaur but the entire situation concerning British tank design.

Battle Cromwell

In February 1944 Leyland Motors announced the specification for what they described as the Battle Cromwell, although the official designation was FS, for Final Specification. In essence it was a short catalogue of features (such as the type of Meteor engine and variant of transmission to be used and the practice of welding seams, even on riveted tanks, to enhance structural strength and waterproofing) that would be acceptable for use on active service. In effect this relegated all Cromwells prior to the Mark IV to the scrap heap. However, it set a standard and provided a tank that well-trained crews could rely upon.

Other features adopted at this time were the All-Round Vision cupola for the commander, along with the vane sight and rear smoke emitters. On certain marks an improved type of idler was seen and the perforated tyres were replaced by solids. Stronger trackguards and lockers were fitted, Cromwell-pattern track adjusters were standard and all tanks were

Centaur III Type C being used test Prong, the British version Sergeant Culin's hedgerow tter. Tested in September 44, it was not produced until ovember for Cromwell, which as too late to be of any use.

prepared for deep wading. Evidence from reports suggests that a number of these improvements were not honoured one hundred per cent. Many Cromwells that served in North-West Europe were not up to Final Specification in all respects.

Leyland and Fowlers had now joined the Cromwell Group, but it was still a race against time. Four hundred FS Cromwells were required by D-Day but only 152 had been accepted by April 1944. Some regiments only reached full establishment on the eve of embarkation.

Royal Marines

In an effort to provide Royal Marine Commandos with their own fire support on D-Day, the Marines acquired 80 Centaur 95mm close-support tanks and developed a system of gunnery based upon naval gunfire techniques. The plan was to remove the engines from these tanks and mount them on Tank Landing Craft, raised high enough to fire over the bulwarks. These craft would then operate off the beaches, bringing down fire on Marine objectives as required, and finally run ashore and continue firing from the shoreline. Since this would demand considerable expenditure of ammunition, the vacant engine compartments would be used to store additional rounds.

Then everything changed. Following an exercise on the Dorset coast, General Montgomery suggested it would make more sense for the tanks to land and drive ashore, so engines were refitted and Royal Armoured Corps drivers transferred to the Marines. Formed as the Royal Marine Armoured Support Group, it comprised two armoured regiments, sub-divided in batteries and one Independent Armoured Battery. Denied everything in the way of technical and material support, this gallant band still managed to do extremely well. Some of their distinctively marked Centaurs could still be found, more than two weeks after the initial landings, fighting up to 16km (10 miles) inshore.

When the unit was disbanded their surviving Centaurs were distributed to various units, including one special Canadian battery supporting 6th Airborne Division, before being handed over to the French.

CROMWELL IN ACTION

Reports on the effectiveness of Cromwell on the battlefield are compounded of official wishful thinking, personal loyalty or simple misunderstanding. One commentator, writing in the *Royal Armoured Corps Journal*, reported on the fate of those Cromwells destroyed in the debacle at Villers Bocage on 14 June 1944. The writer describes Cromwell as 'the new British Cruiser tank' but said that its armour was not in the same class as Panthers and Tigers. The fate of some 4th County of London Yeomanry's tanks, he says, was 'a mishap that put the case against British tank design far better than a dozen speeches in Parliament could do'. Cromwell may have been Britain's latest tank, but it was hardly new, and on welded types the frontal armour was exactly the same thickness as

21ST ARMY GROUP AND ALLIED UNITS OPERATING CROMWELL FAMILY AFVS, 1944–45

Formation	Regiments	Tanks	Remarks
Royal Marines Armoured Support Group (RMASG)	1st & 2nd Armoured Support Regiments, RM 5th (Independent) Armoured Support Battery, RM	Centaur IV	Normandy, D-Day to D+14
Free French Forces 51st Highland Division (attached)	13e Régiment des Dragons 6th LAA Battery, 27th Light Anti-Aircraft Regiment, RA	Centaur IV Centaur IV	Ex-RMASG, no combat service Ex-RMASG, until 30/7/44
6th Airborne Division (attached)	(a) 'X' Armoured Battery, 53rd Light Regiment, RA (b) 1st Canadian Centaur Battery, RCA	Centaur IV	Ex-RMASG, transferred to Canadians on 6/8/44
6th Airborne Division	6th Airborne Reconnaissance Regiment	Cromwell	Divisional Recce Regt
7th Armoured Division	8th King's Royal Irish Hussars	Cromwell Challenger	Armoured Recce Regt
7th Armoured Division (22nd Armoured Brigade)	1st Royal Tank Regiment 5th Royal Tank Regiment 4th County of London Yeomanry 5th Royal Inniskillen Dragoon Guards	Cromwell Challenger Comet	4CLY replaced by 5RIDG 8/44 Challenger in 5RTR, 8/44 Comet in 1RTR, Berlin, 9/45
11th Armoured Division	2nd Northants Yeomanry 15/19th Hussars	Cromwell Challenger	Armd Recce Regts 2NY replaced by 15/19H 8/44
11th Armoured Division (29th and 159th Brigade Groups)	15/19th Hussars 123rd Hussars 2nd Fife & Forfar Yeomanry 3rd Royal Tank Regiment	Comet Cromwell Challenger	3/45 to 5/45. Challenger in 15/19H only
Guards Armoured Division	2nd Battalion, Welsh Guards	Cromwell Challenger	Armoured Recce Regt
1st (Polish) Armoured Division	10th (Polish) Mounted Rifles Regiment	Cromwell Challenger	Armoured Recce Regt
1st (Czechoslovakian) Independent Armoured Brigade Group	1st, 2nd and 3rd (Czechoslovakian) Armoured Regiments	Cromwell Challenger	1st Canadian Army, Dunkirk, 9/44 to 5/45
79th Armoured Division. (1st Assault Brigade, RE)	87 Assault Dozer Squadron, Royal Engineers	Centaur Dozer	Germany, 4/45 to 5/45

Tiger. It was the gun that was the problem. In fact, given precisely the same circumstances, no tanks could have survived what happened outside Villers Bocage, not even if 4th CLY themselves had been equipped with Tigers.

The best sources of operational information on Cromwell are 21st Army Group Technical Reports. The Cromwell had few chances to show its spurs until the Great Swan, the amazing dash across France to Belgium.

This scruffy-looking Cromwell IV Type E is of no significance in itself except that it was used, at the end of WWII, to test a British version of the German Zimmerit anti-magnetic paste. Apparently the stuff came off in chunks every time it was hit.

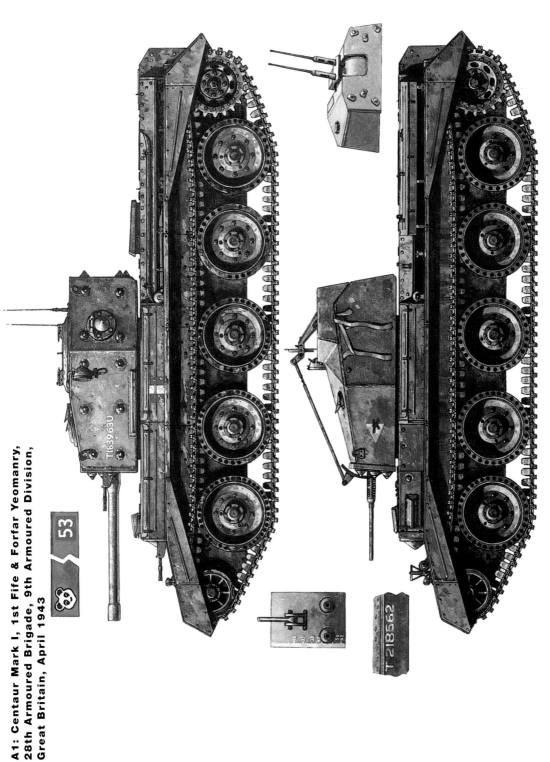

A1: Centaur Mark I, 1st Fife & Forfar Yeomanry, 28th Armoured Brigade, 9th Armoured Division, Great Britain, April 1943

A2: Centaur III AA Tank Mark I, Great Britain, 1944

B: Centaur Mark IV, No. 2 Battery, 1st Regiment,
Royal Marine Armoured Support Group, Normandy,
June 1944

B

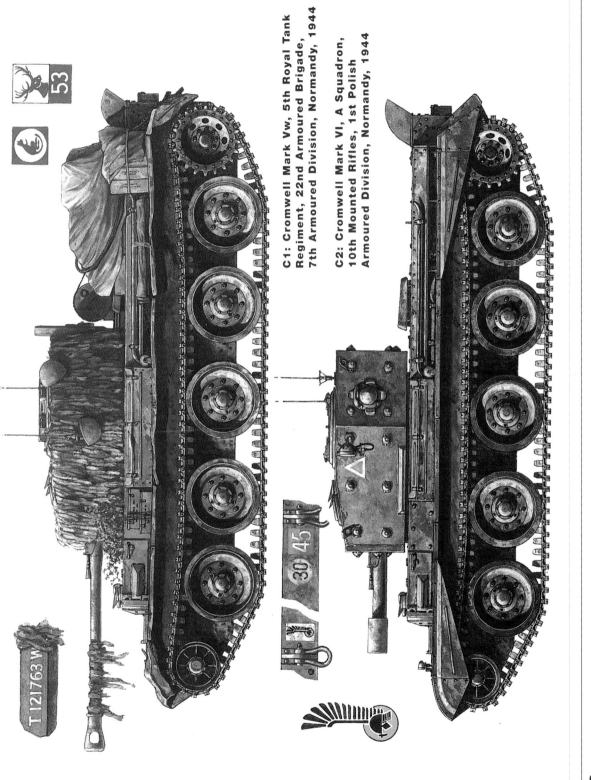

C1: Cromwell Mark Vw, 5th Royal Tank Regiment, 22nd Armoured Brigade, 7th Armoured Division, Normandy, 1944

C2: Cromwell Mark VI, A Squadron, 10th Mounted Rifles, 1st Polish Armoured Division, Normandy, 1944

D: CROMWELL TANK

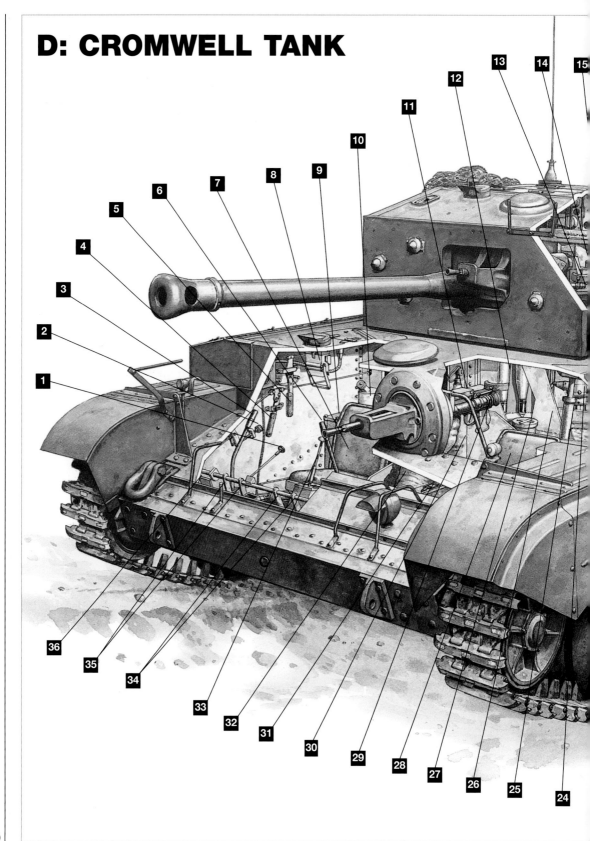

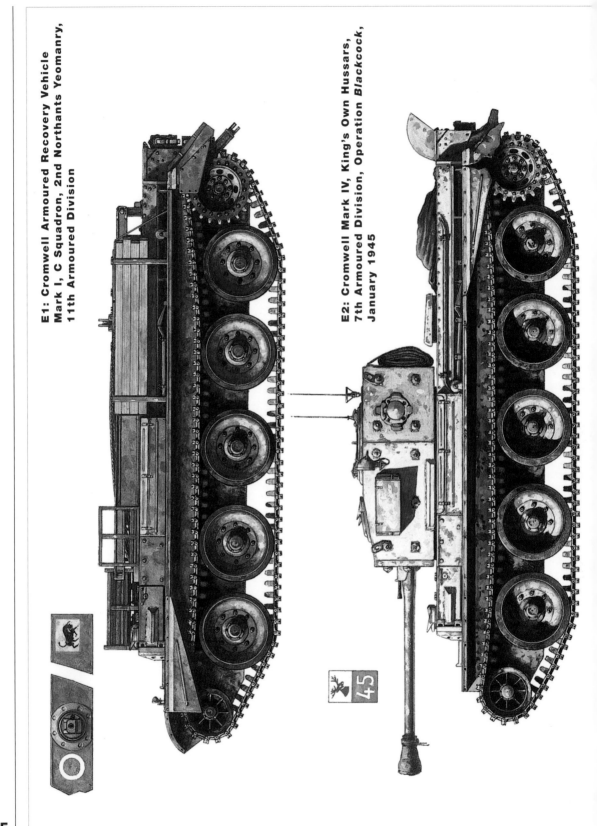

E1: Cromwell Armoured Recovery Vehicle Mark I, C Squadron, 2nd Northants Yeomanry, 11th Armoured Division

E2: Cromwell Mark IV, King's Own Hussars, 7th Armoured Division, Operation *Blackcock*, January 1945

F: A34 Comet, Regimental Headquarters, 2nd Fife & Forfar Yeomanry, 11th Armoured Division, Germany, 1945

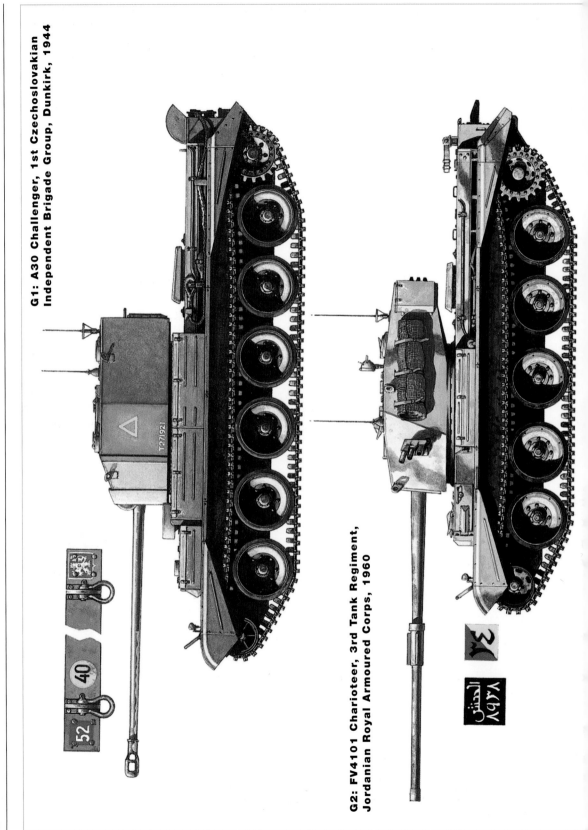

G1: A30 Challenger, 1st Czechoslovakian Independent Brigade Group, Dunkirk, 1944

G2: FV4101 Charioteer, 3rd Tank Regiment, Jordanian Royal Armoured Corps, 1960

G

The tank was praised for its reliability, the only major problem being road-wheel tyres that began to crumble under the strain. A shortage of spare road wheels led to some units cannibalizing their Crusader AA tanks, so Cromwells began to appear with a mixture of solid and perforated tyres.

The autumn of 1944 saw a return to positional warfare, with engines overheating as mud and fallen leaves clogged air intakes. This malfunction was made worse where crews piled on extra stowage that masked air intakes, until they were ordered to stop.

Mines were also a menace and Cromwells seem to have been particularly vulnerable; the explosion could twist a hull out of alignment, causing the tank to be written off. Mine blast would also buckle trackguards, jamming hatches and preventing escape. The Czech Brigade solved this by fitting tack-welded panels instead of trackguards; these would simply break off, leaving the hatch clear. The practice of welding spare track links to tanks as additional protection was popular, but frowned upon as ineffective by experts. Yet there is evidence of one Cromwell IV surviving five direct hits from a 75mm PaK 40 at 274m (300yd) while a nearby tank, without such protection, was knocked out.

WARTIME VARIANTS AND SPECIALIST VEHICLES

Command and Control Tanks

The Royal Armoured Corps half-yearly report for the first half of 1944 lists Command, Control, Rear Link and OP (Observation Post) variants of Cromwell. It is a complicated subject to cover in a few words but, according to a table issued in 1943 these different Cromwell variants were fitted out as follows:

CAVALIER, CENTAUR, CROMWELL AND COMET HULL TYPES

CAVALIERS, CENTAURS, AND RIVETED CROMWELLS

Type	Description	Applicable to:
A	Two escape hatches in driving compartment roof, belly escape hatch, four trackguard stowage lockers. Hull floor plate 6mm (0.24in) thick with additional spaced, 8mm (0.31in) layer below crew compartments. No 20 gimbal mounting for hull BESA with No 35 periscopic gunsight and separate vision periscope for hull gunner. Long-range fuel tank optional. Engine deck air intake standard on Cromwells and optional on Centaurs, depending on manufacturer.	Cavalier I Cromwell I, III and X
B	Side escape hatch for hull gunner. Belly escape hatch deleted. Three trackguard stowage lockers. No 20 gimbal or No 21 ball mounting for hull BESA. Hull gunner's vision periscope deleted. Long-range fuel tank optional.	Cavalier I Centaur I
C	Similar to Type B but engine compartment armour reduced and long-range fuel tank deleted to save weight. New pattern of engine deck air intake for all Cromwells and some Centaurs. No 20 gimbal or No 21 ball mounting for hull BESA. Hull gunner's vision periscope reinstated on later vehicles. Revised trackguards introduced on later Cromwell IVCs.	Centaur I, III and IV Cromwell I, III, IV, V and VI
D	Similar to Type C but engine deck redesigned to improve access to radiators. No 21 ball mounting for hull BESA, hull gunner's vision periscope and revised trackguards all standard.	Centaur III and IV Cromwell IV and VI
E	Similar to Type D but laminated floor plate replaced by a single-skin 14mm (0.55in) floor plate.	Cromwell IV and VI
F	Similar to Type E, but with driver's side escape hatch. Two trackguard stowage lockers. Two turret side stowage lockers. Towing ropes stowed on glacis plate. Late vehicles had WD Pattern sprung drawbar for guns and trailers. All Type F had Cromwell suspension as standard.	Cromwell IV and VI

Continued on page 34

Cromwell Command Tank. One each No 19 Low Power (LP) and High Power (HP) wireless sets with the main armament removed. These were issued at divisional and brigade HQ level.

Cromwell Control Tank. Two LP sets, armament and ammunition retained. Issued at regimental HQ level.

Cromwell Rear Link Tank. One HP set with armament and ammunition retained. Issued to HQ of armoured reconnaissance regiments.

Cromwell Observation Post (OP) Tank. Two No 19 and two No 38 portable sets, armour and ammunition retained. Issued to artillery regiments in armoured division and armoured brigade HQs.

Later came Contact Tanks, converted in the field. These were equipped with one No 19 Command set, one No 19 Air Support Signals Unit (ASSU) set and a VHF set. Used by RAF liaison officers to control fighter-bombers, they also had a dummy gun and were fitted with telescopic aerials taken from captured German equipment.

Armoured Recovery Vehicle

Outwardly it can be difficult to distinguish a Cromwell ARV from the Cavalier version, especially when fully stowed with recovery equipment, although the obvious differences in terms of engine, transmission and rear-end arrangements are there. Records show that 58 Cromwell ARVs had been delivered by the end of 1944 but these were not new construction. They were converted from existing gun tanks, usually Mark IV Cromwells with Type C hulls.

AA tanks

Tanks fitted with anti-aircraft guns to provide air defence for armoured formations were not a new idea, but experience in France in 1940 stimulated development and, following experience with Light Tanks, this became a Cruiser Tank role that devolved upon the Crusader (see New Vanguard 14). Centaur was regarded as the natural successor and in

omwell T187820 was a Mark IV
ɔe E issued to the Specialized
nour Development
tablishment (SADE) and is
re being used to test a
rsion of the Canadian
destructible Roller Device
RD), which has pulled the
ntre of gravity well forward.

October 1943 a prototype was inspected. It was similar to the Crusader AA Tank Mark III, but with Polsten cannon replacing the 20mm Oerlikons of the former. Since the turret was cramped, and liable to quite violent movement in action, the wireless set with its operator was installed in the hull. In Crusader the AA turret was powered by the tank's engine, but the Centaur employed an auxiliary generator located in the nose of the tank with its own exhaust pipe situated on the nearside trackguard.

No reason has ever been found to explain why Centaur AA tanks should not have replaced the unreliable Crusaders with the armoured divisions in Europe. However, by October 1944 the order for Centaur AA tanks Mark I had been cut back from 450 to 100 and its replacement, the Mark II, probably only existed as a single example. The Mark II mounted an enlarged turret that included an extra man, a gunner, sitting alongside the tank commander who now tracked the target for him. There are hints that Centaur AA tanks were employed as part of Operation *Diver*, the concentrated AA barrage mounted as an antidote to the V1 flying bombs. But if true, where they were deployed and who operated them is not known. There is one report of a Centaur AA Mark III, which also existed in prototype form and featured a new design of turret. All of these improvements went by the board when the AA tank programme was cut back.

Centaur Dozer

The demise of the anti-aircraft tank programme was followed quickly by a revival of interest in armoured bulldozer tanks. The Crusader had been tested in this role but found wanting, while the Centaur, with its greater weight, proved far more effective. Built on the hulls of redundant AA tanks, the Centaur Dozers mounted a full-width blade that was raised and lowered by a powered winch in the fighting compartment via cables running over a small jib at the front. The driver sat in his usual place while the vehicle commander occupied the position on his left, covered by an armoured conning tower.

The War Office requirement for 250 machines was met by MG Cars of Abingdon, who undertook the conversion. The Dozers were issued to 87 Assault Squadron Royal Engineers in 79th Armoured Division and they were used primarily for clearing rubble in bombed and shelled built-up areas. Even so, deliveries were slow and they did not

ken from the special tower at
e Lulworth Gunnery School,
is top view of A30 Challenger
ows how the central part of
e hull had to be enlarged to
ke the bigger turret. Notice
so how far forward the
mmander's cupola is located.

Detail view of an A30 Challenger in service showing both turret hatches open and the curved strip of armour that protected the turret ring at the front. No unit details are available beyond the fact that the turret insignia suggests 4 Troop in C Squadron; a system typical of 15/19th Hussars.

go operational until April 1945. Centaur Dozers later saw service in the Korean War and even the 1956 Suez crisis, in Operation *Musketeer*.

Centaur Kangaroos, described as turretless personnel carriers, are mentioned at the end of the war. Some details also survive of a Royal Electrical and Mechanical Engineers (REME) programme to produce gutted, turretless personnel carriers to be towed, full of troops, behind battle tanks. A redundant Cromwell was converted in France, with engine doors from a Sherman tank fitted at the back, but a plan to modify Centaurs in the UK was dropped.

Drawings survive for other Cromwell projects, including one with an exposed, multiple machine-gun mounting and even a self-propelled gun with a 25-pdr in an enclosed structure. These were never built, but other experimental modifications will be found among the photographs.

A30 Challenger

The origins of Challenger are open to various interpretations. The official line is that BRCW were asked to design a new tank 'with the minimum amount of design and development that would carry the 17 pounder gun'. On the other hand W.A. Robotham, then chief engineer at the Department of Tank Design, later claimed that it was his idea and that the design work was carried out by his Rolls-Royce team at Belper in Derbyshire. There may be an element of truth in both claims, but on balance one tends to favour the official line since there is more hard evidence to back it up.

It is that phrase about the minimum amount of design and development that should set the alarm bells ringing, yet it appears to have been British policy for tank design since 1940. Perfectly reasonable too, if one is improving upon the best, but not when it involves taking a short cut that results in something less than adequate. The matter was not improved by handing parts of the design to different firms in the hope that they could be made to harmonize afterwards. Thus work on the turret was entrusted to Stothert & Pitt of Bath, a

One of a series of classic pictures showing a Challenger of 4 Troop, C Squadron, 15/19th Hussars in Holland in October 1944. Considerable effort has been made to camouflage both gun and turret, which seems only to emphasize its apparent bulk.

87820 again, with CIRD brackets at the front, now modified to carry and fire four 82mm (3in) Typhoon rockets with 27kg (60lb) warheads. This was another SADE trial, staged in 1946.

firm that normally specialized in the manufacture of large cranes, while BRCW developed the chassis to receive it. This would be the big short cut since it was a modification to the A27M hull, which had to be enlarged to carry a bigger and much heavier turret.

The essential requirement was to increase the diameter of the turret ring from 1524mm (60in) on the Cromwell to 1778mm (70in), and this was done by creating a new central superstructure, elevated above the level of the engine deck and extended outwards over the tracks. The design team also deemed it necessary to extend the tank to accommodate the new superstructure and reduce the ground pressure (on account of the greater weight) by putting more track on the ground. Since the hull had to be stretched, an extra wheel station was added on each side to support it. Lengthening a tank without widening it in proportion invariably leads to steering difficulties, but widening this tank ran the unacceptable risk of exceeding the British railway loading gauge, which had inhibited the design of British tanks since 1916.

Stothert & Pitt's turret was enormous, not just to accommodate the big gun but to leave enough headroom for the elevation and depression demanded by the War Office. Since the extra weight of this part-cast and part-welded turret could have been prohibitive the entire turret assembly rested upon a large steel ball, held in a special cradle on the hull floor to avoid the complication of a conventional ball race turret ring.

The ball device (described as a 'doubtful blessing' by one commentator) assisted with a secondary function unique (unless one

Another SADE trial, a development of the wartime Canal Defence Light scheme, now this Mark VIIw mounting a pair of mercury-vapour spotlights at the front. For experimental purposes power was supplied by two generators mounted on the rear deck.

includes the heavy tank TOG 2) to Challenger. This was the ability, from inside the fighting compartment, to jack up the turret by up to 25.4mm (1in). The idea was that the risk of it jamming through accidental damage or enemy action could be obviated by raising the turret sufficiently to clear the problem and then lowering it again.

Tank Board representatives saw the prototype A30 at Farnborough in August 1942. It was an ungainly looking thing with the tall, solid turret dominating a long, low hull. Gunnery trials at Lulworth revealed that the new Metropolitan Vickers Metadyne electric turret traverse gear worked very well, but it was suggested that a second loader would be a sensible idea due to the weight of the projectile. In the event it seems that on active service the extra loader was dispensed with, and certainly other 17-pdr armed vehicles managed with just the one. The turret carried a co-axial machine gun that, oddly for a British tank at that time, was the .30-calibre (7.62mm) Browning, but there was no machine gun in the hull. Space in the new tank was at a premium, particularly for ammunition stowage, but it also saved weight.

By February 1943 A30 had been accepted for production and an order for 200 placed with BRCW, with the proviso that they took precedence over Cromwell production. Challenger's role was a specialized one: to provide long-range anti-tank support for the Cromwells in its regiment and not to replace them, as Montgomery seems to have believed at one time.

A view inside the Birmingham Railway Carriage & Wagon Company works at Smethwick, Birmingham, showing A30 Avenger hulls on the production line with turrets waiting in the adjoining bay.

Into action

Challenger, like its more popular rival the Sherman Firefly, was described at the time as a hole puncher (the holes being in other people's tanks). On paper at least it could defeat 111mm (4.37in) of armour at ranges up to 1,828m (2,000yd) firing APCBC ammunition, but when firing APDS that figure went up to 161mm (6.34in). In practice it seems the gun was not as accurate as it might have been and the sights no better than average. Some suggest that the round could wobble in flight and ricochet from an oblique strike when it should have smashed straight through. It is also worth recalling what the Experimental Wing of the Gunnery School at Lulworth said of Challenger that 'under European conditions the performance at long ranges of the 17-pounder gun could not be relied on as a compensating factor for inadequate armour protection'. Even so the gun was regarded with a healthy respect by German tank crews.

In the interests of uniformity Challengers were only issued to Cromwell-equipped regiments in North-West Europe, starting with 15/19th Hussars in August 1944. Limited operational use revealed a weakness in the front idler assembly that resulted in the whole lot being withdrawn for a while. Half way through production other changes were introduced, notably increased armour protection to front-facing surfaces. In 1943 plans had been drawn up for a 36.6-tonne (36-ton) Challenger Stage II with heavier armour to General Staff specification, but the project was abandoned.

A30 Avenger SP2

In British service tank destroyers were the province of the Royal Artillery who operated the American M10, re-armed with a 17-pdr gun, and the Valentine Archer equipped with the same weapon, this last as an interim measure. Although a contemporary of the Archer in terms of design, A30 17-pounder SP (the name Avenger was not adopted until after the war) took longer to evolve. Essentially it was a low-profile version of the A30 Challenger's hull with a 17-pdr in an equally low turret that was open at the top. Following experience in North-West Europe, where the Germans employed air-burst shells to harm tank destroyer crews, the turret of Avenger, also known as SP2, was fitted with a spaced head cover. It was an impressive-looking machine, but arrived too late to see operational service and only served briefly with two anti-tank regiments when hostilities were over. The Royal Artillery Wing at Bovington Camp ceased teaching Avenger after 1949.

A34 Comet

Although it was too large to fit Cromwell, development of Vickers' 50-calibre, high-velocity 75mm gun continued. However, to confuse the issue, by the time it entered service the calibre had changed to 76.2mm, the breech modified to accept 17-pdr ammunition while the official description altered to 77mm, to distinguish it from the longer weapon fitted to Challenger. The new gun proved to be more accurate than the 17-pdr when firing HE rounds. Despite this the Tank Board at one point suggested that the new American 76mm gun should be considered. Fortunately, since this weapon failed to live up to expectations, the final choice of the new British gun helped to make Comet an excellent tank.

Leyland Motors was appointed manufacturing Parent, having evidently overcome their suspicion of the Meteor engine. Indeed in most respects, apart from the turret, Comet was little more than an improved Cromwell – proving that, if the job was done properly, a mediocre British tank could be improved. The result was impressive. The turret was a welded structure with an unusual cast front of quite complex shape containing an external mantlet recessed within the turret ring. There was an extension at the rear to contain the radio and counter-balance the heavier gun. An All-Round Vision cupola was fitted as standard, as were return rollers to support the top run of the wider (457mm – 18in) tracks. Subsequent trials

Photographed on parade with 3rd Royal Tank Regiment in Hong Kong, this Mark I Comet has its War Department registration on the side and a local registration marking on the front. This picture was taken in an era when Britain maintained garrisons in many parts of the world.

suggested that these served no useful purpose at all, but they do help to identify the tank.

Issued first to 29th Armoured Brigade in 11th Armoured Division, Comet soon proved popular, even to crews with long experience of the Sherman. It was fast, manoeuvrable and above all it could fight. It was like having an entire regiment of Fireflies, easily a match for the Panther and perfectly capable of dealing with the Tiger at most ranges.

There is no hard evidence for the existence of Command and Control Comets before the end of the war, although regimental COs certainly used Comets and surviving post-war documents include illustrations to show the turret interior fittings of an official Command and Control Comet.

Comet Crocodile

One surviving photograph reveals the existence of a Comet flame-thrower similar to the Churchill Crocodile, with a pressurized fuel trailer and flame projector mounted in place of the hull machine gun: almost certainly a post-war conversion. No documents have been discovered, but it would be in keeping with Montgomery's views on the Capital tank and his belief that all such tanks should be adaptable to tasks like flame-throwing, mine clearance or amphibious operations. This apart, no other special modifications of the Comet are known.

POST-WAR DEVELOPMENTS

The place of Cromwell and Comet in the post-war world might be summed up, as far as the British Army was concerned, in a Fighting Vehicle Design Establishment (FVDE) report *c.*1950 in which the two tanks were marked down as vulnerable at all ranges to every Russian anti-tank weapon from the old 76mm gun of the T-34 upwards. Nevertheless Comets served with many Territorial Army regiments up to 1954; many of these tanks were stockpiled in the Middle East.

Fearnaught was a Comet of Headquarters Squadron, 6th Royal Tank Regiment, which was converted to the command role with a dummy 95mm gun, a weapon never actually fitted to Comet. The tank was photographed on a rail flat in Italy, just after the war.

Surviving, original Marks and Types			Not Reworked to later Marks	Reworked Cromwells				Cromwell Totals	Converted to Charioteers				Charioteer Totals
Manufacturer	Mark	Type		Mark 4D	Mark 7	Mark 7w	Mark 8		Mark 6	Mark 7	Mark 7w	Mark 8	
RCW Co. Ltd	I	A	1	0	0	0	0	1	0	0	0	0	0
	I	C	1	0	0	0	0	1	0	0	0	0	0
	V, NFS	C	13	0	29	0	0	42	0	2	0	0	2
	Vw, FS	Dw	5	0	0	7	0	12	0	0	5	0	5
	Vw, FS	Ew	3	0	0	0	0	3	0	0	0	0	0
	VIIw, FS	Ew	36	0	0	0	0	36	0	0	36	0	36
English-Electric	IV, NFS	C	26	2	19	0	0	47	0	0	0	0	0
	IV, FS	C	1	77	65	0	0	143	0	40	0	0	40
Fowler	VI, FS	D	1	0	0	0	2	3	0	0	0	2	2
	VI, FS	E	36	1	0	0	17	54	1	0	0	17	18
Leyland etc.	IV, FS	E	50	0	87	0	0	137	0	60	0	0	60
	IV, FS	F	189	0	225	0	0	414	0	154	0	0	154
Metropolitan-Cammell	VI, NFS	C	0	0	0	0	5	5	0	0	0	0	0
	VI, NFS	D	5	0	0	0	2	7	0	0	0	0	0
	VI, FS	D	13	0	0	0	11	24	3	0	0	11	14
	VI, FS	E	13	0	0	0	14	27	2	0	0	14	16
	VI, FS	F	98	0	5	0	50	153	38	5	0	52	95
Grand Totals			491	80	430	7	101	1109	44	261	41	96	442

However there were still Cromwells to spare and many of these were subject to a major rework scheme intended to bring surviving earlier Marks up to date. A total of 618 were rebuilt by the Royal Ordnance factories and 442 later converted to Charioteer. Note that from 1948, when a new War Department registration system was introduced, the British Army ceased to use Roman numerals for Mark designations and switched to Arabic. Thus, for example, a wartime Cromwell Vw might be reworked to appear as a Mark 7w.

Probably the last Cromwells to fire their guns in anger with British forces were those of the reconnaissance troop of 8th King's Royal Irish Hussars and 45th Field Regiment Royal Artillery (gun-armed OP tanks) in a desperate action against overwhelming odds in January 1951, during the Korean War. Comets lasted a good deal longer, but were never called upon to engage in any serious action. A few long-term survivors were used for experimental purposes, the most significant being the installation of an externally mounted 83.8mm auto-loading gun, developed by the Fighting Vehicle Research and Development Establishment in 1968 under the name COMRES-75.

FV4101 Charioteer

Early in 1951 the Director, Royal Armoured Corps, Major-General Nigel Duncan, announced that in the event of hostilities, presumably against Russia, it would be necessary to employ Cromwell tanks in at least one formation. DRAC was fully aware that the tank's 75mm gun was impotent against contemporary Russian tanks and had requested that the FVDE see if they could find a way of mounting the 83.4mm 20-pdr gun on the A27M. It was a tall order.

We have already seen the problems involved in fitting the 17-pdr, and the 20-pdr, which first appeared in 1947, was even bigger. It had been

CROMWELL FAMILY: OVERSEAS DELIVERIES & SALES, 1943–72							
	Cavalier	Centaur	Cromwell	Challenger	Comet	Charioteer	Totals	Notes
Australia			1				1	Evaluation vehicle
Austria						82	82	
Burma					22		22	
Cuba					14		14	
Czechoslovakia			168	22			190	Ex-1st (Czechoslovakian) Armd Bde
Eire					8		8	
Finland					41	38	79	
France	43	71					114	Including some Cavalier OPs
Greece		52					52	
Hong Kong					69		69	Hong Kong garrison
Israel		2					2	Stolen from 4/7 Dragoon Guards, 1948
Jordan						49	49	1967 War survivors sold to Lebanon
Lebanon						20	20	Excludes ex-Jordanian vehicles
Portugal		n/a					n/a	Not available
South Africa					26		26	
USSR		6					6	Evaluation vehicles
West Germany					13		13	
Grand Totals	**43**	**123**	**177**	**22**	**193**	**189**	**747**	

developed for the Centurion Mark 3 but Centurion production was in arrears so there were guns to spare. The most remarkable thing about the new design was the way in which FVDE managed to widen the hull above the fighting compartment to accommodate a larger turret ring without having to extend it. This meant that the basic Cromwell hull remained intact so that performance and reliability were not affected, but the overall result was dreadful.

The new turret was enormous, and to keep the weight down frontal armour was a mere 38mm (1.5in) and the sides just 25mm (1in). This was not a tank in which the crew would be given a second chance. As for the crew, they originally numbered three: driver, loader/radio operator and commander/gunner. This is why, according to some, the turret does not feature a commander's cupola – in action neither he nor his loader had any time to look out. The loader had enough to do handling the large rounds, although there were only 25 of them, of which three were held on clips in the turret itself. When he was neither loading nor operating the radio, the loader could fire the co-axial machine gun mounted to the left of the main armament. There was no machine gun in the hull; the space to the left of the driver was earmarked for the crews' personal kit, although sometimes a fourth man travelled here. The 20-pdr's muzzle blast could obscure the target below 1,371m (1,500yd), so the commander would dismount and direct fire from the flank while this fourth man took his place as gunner.

Charioteer was also described as an anti-tank gun and it had a lot in common with the previous generation of tank destroyers, except that the turret was fully enclosed. However, the addition of a co-axial machine gun should qualify it as a tank and that was certainly how it was perceived when it first entered service with Territorial Army regiments of the Royal Armoured Corps. Even so, its service with the British Army was short and many were exported, as shown in the table at the top of the page.

A Cromwell V Type C, reworked to Cromwell 7 Type D for post-war service in the Middle East. The SA serial was normally issued to tanks that did not qualify for FS (Final Specification). The crew are chatting to the locals, but the tank is not mounting its machine guns.

...ipoli is a Cromwell VIII Type F ...at started life as a Cromwell ... It is shown here in company ...ith Comets of 40th Royal ...nk Regiment (23rd Armoured ...rigade) on parade in ...verpool. Later still this ...nk became a Charioteer ...ee photo on page 45).

There are two instances of Charioteer being up-gunned to take the 105mm weapon that had replaced the 20-pdr in Centurion. Trials at Shoeburyness and Kirkcudbright in 1960 showed that despite the extra recoil force, believed to be too strong for such a light hull, the gun worked well with no detrimental effect. A British Army team sent out to the Lebanon in 1972 to examine a 105mm Charioteer apparently converted out there – using electric, instead of hydraulic, turret traverse – found the tank in such a poor state of repair that no sensible results could be achieved.

Comet 1 Armoured Maintenance Vehicle

Almost certainly the last manifestation of Comet in a service role was the Armoured Maintenance Vehicle employed by the Army of the Republic of South Africa. Note the word 'maintenance' as distinct from 'recovery'. The Comet AMV prototype was developed by the Orange Free State Command Workshops at Bloemfontein in 1978. Once this vehicle had been evaluated it became one of three Comet AMVs to enter service with the South African Army in 1980. It was a dramatic conversion with a Continental V-12 air-cooled engine linked to an Allison three-speed automatic gearbox replacing the original drive train. The turretless tank had a crew of four, a powerful Hydrovane hydraulic crane at the rear and a cradle capable of carrying a spare Continental diesel engine for the Olifant tank, South Africa's extensively modified Centurion. In addition to a range of tools, lubricants and water, the AMV carried welding and cutting equipment and its role was clearly to undertake maintenance on disabled Olifants in the field; it probably lacked the stamina to recover one in the usual way. The Comets were retired in 1985 when new, wheeled Armoured Maintenance Vehicles entered service.

...nce a Cromwell IV Type E, ...eworked to a Mark 7 and now ...n abandoned wreck in Korea in ...ompany with a Churchill Mark 7 ...f 7th Royal Tank Regiment.

CONCLUSION

In a clearing alongside a road in Thetford Forest, a Cromwell tank can be found, perched on a brick plinth. It is a memorial to the 7th Armoured Division, the Desert Rats, who trained in this area in the months leading up to D-Day in 1944.

Sitting up there in the weather the tank looks small, with its narrow tracks and box-like turret; it does not dominate the scene, as some of its larger American or German contemporaries might. And yet it did the job.

The bizarre-looking COMRES-7 vehicle on a Comet IB chassis. Ammunition is stowed in tubes, either side of the gun, and passed through an auto-loader at the back. The crew all remai inside the hull. The tank was part of an Anglo-German proje of the 1970s that did not last very long.

There is an old country saying that applies to almost any implement – that it is not the tool but 'the man behind un' that counts. This must be true of the Cromwell; it underwent a long period of preparation to the point that it was virtually out of date when it first went into action. Yet it led three British and one Polish armoured divisions, and a Czech brigade to victory in Europe. Good or bad this must be due in no small part to 'the men behind un'.

BIBLIOGRAPHY

Courage, G., *History of the 15th/19th King's Royal Hussars 1939–1945*, Gale & Polden: 1949

Fitzroy, Olivia, *Men of Valour (VIIIth Hussars) 1929–1957*, private publication: 1961

Jones, Keith, *Sixty Four Days of a Normandy Summer*, St Edmundsbury Press: 1990

Miller, Charles, *History of the 13th/18th (Queen Mary's Own) Hussars 1927–1947*, Chrisman Bradshaw: 1949

Robotham, W. A., *Silver Ghost and Silver Dawn*, Constable: 1970

Taylor, Daniel, *Villers-Bocage Through the Lens*, After the Battle: 1999

Poor but rare picture of Charioteer in British service. Bulled up almost to Red Square standards it is serving with 23rd Armoured Brigade during a parade through Liverpool. It is probably 46th (Liverpool Welsh) Royal Tank Regiment.

COLOUR PLATE COMMENTARY

A1: CENTAUR MARK I, 1ST FIFE & FORFAR YEOMANRY, 28TH ARMOURED BRIGADE, 9TH ARMOURED DIVISION, GREAT BRITAIN, APRIL 1943

This Centaur I, built by English-Electric of Stafford, exhibits the Type A hull, with stowage boxes extending right to the front of the upper hull on both sides. The air-intake cover behind the turret is more typical of Cromwell tanks, though it was seen on this maker's Centaurs as well. The red/white/red flash on the side, more common in the desert

ABOVE Cromwell VIII (see photo on page 43) in its new guise as Charioteer 01ZW29. From this angle the turret looks perfectly reasonable while the 20-pdr gun appears positively massive. External stowage has not been fitted; normally there would be a towing cable at the front and camouflage netting on the sides of the turret, but the barrel clamp, used to secure the gun when the turret is reversed, is visible at the back of the hull. This tank ultimately went to Jordan.

BELOW Photographed in the Taw estuary in North Devon, with Appledore across the water, this Charioteer, with Type A barrel, is on Deep Wading trials at the Combined Operations Experimental Establishment (COXE). The turret crew are taking no chances – both men wear life jackets.

and Italy, was an identification mark later replaced by the white star in Europe.

The distinctive Panda's head device of 9th Armoured Division was never seen outside the United Kingdom, but 1st Fife & Forfar later converted to Crocodile flame-throwers and served as part of 79th Armoured Division. The red square with 53 in white indicates the junior regiment in the armoured brigade.

A2: CENTAUR III AA TANK MARK I, GREAT BRITAIN, 1944

According to contemporary reports Centaurs were due to replace Crusader tanks in the anti-aircraft role in time for the invasion of Europe, but this never happened. Markings shown here are therefore limited to the War Department number, a graduated scale on the mantlet and the symbol, a black cannon on the Royal Armoured Corps colours of the Gunnery School, Lulworth Camp, Dorset.

In addition to the gunner/commander the turret contained two loaders who sat in very cramped positions, vulnerable to injury from the rapidly moving guns and the difficulty of handling large ammunition drums in confined spaces. Thus the No 19 wireless set was located close to the driver and the aerial base may be seen on the glacis plate. Directly behind it is the exhaust pipe for the auxiliary generator, which was also situated close to the driver's position. Rate of fire per gun was 450 rounds per minute.

B: CENTAUR MARK IV, NO. 2 BATTERY, 1ST REGIMENT, ROYAL MARINE ARMOURED SUPPORT GROUP, NORMANDY, JUNE 1944

The most striking feature of these tanks has always been the distinctive turret markings, graduated in degrees of the compass, which were a relic of the original plan to shoot from landing craft operating off-shore. The gunner's periscope was replaced by an artillery sight projecting through an armoured box located ahead of the commander's position. Each regiment comprised two batteries, each of four troops. Each troop included four 95mm Centaurs and a Sherman command tank. Individual troops were identified by letter and tank names were selected to match, usually those of Royal Navy warships, HMS *Hunter* being an H Class destroyer.

Hull machine guns were removed – they would have been useless on board ship. Extra stowage indicates the extent to which this unit had to function entirely on its own resources once ashore.

C1: CROMWELL MARK VW, 5TH ROYAL TANK REGIMENT, 22ND ARMOURED BRIGADE, 7TH ARMOURED DIVISION, NORMANDY, 1944

Typical of veteran Desert Rats, this tank is seriously cluttered with additional stores and also displays one version of the foliage-style turret camouflage adopted during the hedgerow fighting in Normandy. This tank also sports the so-called 'Normandy Cowl', a device to prevent exhaust fumes from cycling back through the turret when the tank was idling.

The battered state of this Cromwell's trackguards would be entirely typical of a tank that had come a long way with its crew. Made of light-gauge metal to save weight, they were easily damaged by enemy fire or driving incidents. At this stage in the war (from November 1944) 5th RTR was the junior armoured regiment in the brigade (No 53) below 5th Dragoon Guards and 1st RTR.

C2: CROMWELL MARK VI, A SQUADRON, 10TH MOUNTED RIFLES, 1ST POLISH ARMOURED DIVISION, NORMANDY, 1944

The 10th Mounted Rifles was divisional reconnaissance regiment to 1st Polish Armoured, hence the white squadron sign. Each squadron would include two 95mm close-support tanks. Organized along the lines of a typical British armoured division of the time, 1st Polish had three regiments of Sherman tanks in the armoured brigade and Cromwells (with A30 Challengers) only in the reconnaissance regiment.

The Poles used their armour with considerable verve. In debatable areas they tended to advance with all guns blazing, giving adjacent British units the impression that some terrible battle was taking place nearby.

D: CROMWELL TANK

See plate for full details.

E1: CROMWELL ARMOURED RECOVERY VEHICLE MARK I, C SQUADRON, 2ND NORTHANTS YEOMANRY, 11TH ARMOURED DIVISION

Again the squadron symbol being in white indicates that 2nd Northamptonshire Yeomanry was acting as divisional reconnaissance regiment for 11th Armoured. This would be the only regiment in the division to be equipped with Cromwells and each squadron had one ARV.

When not in use the jib and hoist were stowed upon the vehicle along with many other items required for recovery operations. Since these vehicles were not equipped with power winches they used snatch blocks and holdfasts to recover the casualty and then tow it to a location from which it could be carried away by a tank transporter. The ARV was manned by REME, the Royal Electrical and Mechanical Engineers.

E2: CROMWELL MARK IV, KING'S OWN HUSSARS, 7TH ARMOURED DIVISION, OPERATION *BLACKCOCK*, JANUARY 1945

Operation *Blackcock* involved some bitter fighting in harsh winter conditions around the Dutch/German border. Tanks were given a rough coating of whitewash to reduce contrast with the snowy landscape and this obliterated virtually all

ABOVE **Excellent shot of a Centaur Mark I Type B at speed. It is demonstrating the effect of its rear smoke emitters at Porton Down on Salisbury Plain in May 1944.**

BELOW **A Centaur with Type A hull being used to test the new 95mm howitzer (without its counterweight). Notice the one perforated-tyre road wheel and the air intake, behind the turret, more typical of a Cromwell.**

markings. The 7th Armoured Division was the only one to be equipped primarily with Cromwell tanks.

Although 8th Hussars were nominally the division reconnaissance regiment they had, by the winter 1945, effectively become a fourth armoured regiment 22nd Armoured Brigade, which reflected experience in the field. This Cromwell has the Type F hull, which can also be recognized by the small stowage boxes now carried on the turret sides.

F: A34 COMET, REGIMENTAL HEADQUARTERS, 2ND FIFE & FORFAR YEOMANRY, 11TH ARMOURED DIVISION, GERMANY, 1945

The four patron saints of the United Kingdom were represented at RHQ. *Saint Andrew* is shown here appropriately for a Scottish regiment. Although official Command and Control versions of Comet were introduced after the war there is no record of them earlier. However, an extra aerial mounting appears to have been fitted on the glacis plate of *Saint Andrew*, suggesting a field modification. The white 53 indicates that at this time 2nd Fife & Forfar was the junior regiment in 29th Armoured Brigade, a fact also reflected in the blue diamond symbol representing regimental headquarters.

en at Harland & Wolff in Belfast a new Centaur I, still
aiting its armament. This tank has perforated tyres on
road wheels and the Cromwell-type air intake that was
o typical of Centaurs built by English-Electric and
e LMS Railway.

From this low angle the wider (457mm/18in) tracks give the
met a much more solid appearance than its predecessor
e Cromwell. It was better armoured than A27M if not quite
fast, but the 77mm gun could penetrate 122mm (4.8in)
armour at 1,828m (2,000yd) firing APDS and was also
nowned for its accuracy. Unfortunately, Comet arrived on the
ene too late to take full advantage of this.

1: A30 CHALLENGER, 1ST CZECHOSLOVAKIAN INDEPENDENT BRIGADE GROUP, DUNKIRK, 144

uipped entirely with Cromwells and Challengers, apart from
me Stuart reconnaissance tanks, the Czech regiments spent
ost of their time investing the German garrison in the port of
nkirk, which had been by-passed by the main Allied
vance. When hostilities ended the Czechs and their tanks
urned home.

Seen in profile the Challenger looks ungainly, although
fact it had a slightly lower profile than a Sherman. One

problem common to all 17-pdr armed tanks was the length
of the gun, which seemed to attract enemy attention. Among
many attempts to disguise it the method shown, of painting
half of the underside in a paler colour, was the most popular.

G2: FV4101 CHARIOTEER, 3RD TANK REGIMENT, JORDANIAN ROYAL ARMOURED CORPS, 1960

Following service with the British Territorial Army, 189 of the
442 Cromwell tanks converted to Charioteers were sold
abroad. Austria took 82, Finland finished up with 38, Jordan
49 and Lebanon 20. The Jordanian tanks were among the
most potent AFVs in the Middle East when they joined the
Arab Legion in 1954, but they were worse than obsolete by
the time of the 1967 Six-Day War and those that survived the
Israeli counter-attack were passed to Lebanon where,
following their civil war, some were taken over by the
Palestine Liberation Organization.

The artwork shows a Jordanian tank fitted with the B-type
20-pdr (83.4mm/3.28in) gun, identified by the concentric fume
extractor half way down the barrel.

**A Challenger, displaying the additional frontal armour used
on the last hundred tanks to leave Birmingham. Alongside is
the far lower profile of the prototype Avenger Tank Destroyer,
which mounts the same gun in an open-top turret.**

INDEX